Comprehension Lifters

Written by Dr. Sheila Twine

Published by World Teachers Press®

Published with the permission of R.I.C. Publications Pty. Ltd.

First published by R.I.C. Publications Pty. Ltd., Perth, Western Australia.

Printed in the United States of America.

Order Number 2-5125
ISBN 1-58324-049-7

A B C D E F 03 02 01 00

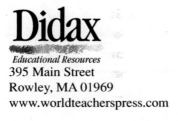

Educational Resources
395 Main Street
Rowley, MA 01969
www.worldteacherspress.com

Foreword

Comprehension Lifters is a set of blackline masters designed to assist students who have experienced difficulties with reading and comprehension. Topics are of high interest to appeal to older students with low literacy skills. Comprehension activities are varied and include superficial and in-depth questions requiring students to interact with text at a range of levels.

The four books of *Comprehension Lifters* can be used on their own or in conjunction with the four books of *Literacy Lifters* by the same author. Thus, students working at a basic level on Book 1 of *Literacy Lifters* would progress to Book 1 of *Comprehension Lifters* before moving on to Book 2 of *Literacy Lifters*.

In both *Literacy Lifters* and *Comprehension Lifters*, the book numbers do not correspond to grade or class levels, but rather to the skill level of students. Books progress in level of difficulty. Thus, Book 1 is aimed at a basic reading level and would be suitable for students who had floundered with their start to literacy. Book 2 would be appropriate for students who require assistance with basic skills. Books 3 and 4 would suit students whose reading and understanding of text is at a low level.

About the Author

Dr. Sheila Twine is an educational consultant who has worked with students with special needs, as well as parents and teachers, in England, Scotland and Australia. She is the author of three books containing practical techniques for working with students who experience difficulties with reading and spelling. She holds a Master's Degree and a Doctorate in Education.

Dr. Twine has been president of various associations and foundations involved with underachieving students with a variety of disabilities from mild developmental delay to attention deficit disorder. She was principal of a residential remedial primary school and has been the director of an education consultancy for many years.

Contents

Teachers Notes

GENERAL LAYOUT

Comprehension Lifters has been designed as a teaching tool to assist you in raising the literacy levels of your students who are experiencing difficulties with reading and comprehension.

The page layout is similar throughout the books with text well separated by pictures to make discouraged readers feel more at ease. Each book has forty topic pages dealing with aspects of the same theme which are intended to be of interest to older students with low literacy skills. The font size is appropriate to the students' ages and so is smaller than normal for the easier reading level; therefore, the pages do not look "babyish."

The **Backing Sheet** can be copied on the back of any or all of the topic pages. It is general and designed to complement your teaching. It contains space for activities in word study, integration and writing.

TOPIC PAGES

Each topic page has a number of sections. There is a section for patterned words which are phonically regular (found, sound, round) and for sight words (the, said, enough) for instant recognition. Most pages also have longer words broken into "chunks" to encourage your students to tackle unfamiliar words more easily (nav-i-gate).

There are many comprehension sections. These include:

Main idea – Students need to be able to grasp the main idea of the text. Selecting or creating a title assists with this and is featured on every topic page.

Cloze activity – Each page also features a cloze activity which requires students to think as they read so a sensible word can be inserted into the blank spaces using clues from the text.

Questions – **Literal** questions are included where the answer is clear from the story. There are also **inferential** questions where students are asked to think and provide a logical answer. (He put on his raincoat – What was the weather like?)

Others – Some pages feature **following directions** or **giving opinions**. Some ask students to **make judgements** and some ask for elements to be put in correct **sequence**.

At the bottom of each topic page there is a section that can act as a challenge for the more able students in your group to read to the others. The section either asks a deeper level of comprehension question or gives more information about the topic.

TEACHING TIPS

Two teaching strategies which were used when the layout of the topic pages was being tested concerned **pre-reading** and **blank-filling**. You may like to try them.

Pre-reading – Students were asked to glance at the pictures on their topic page then turn the page over (so no reading took place). They were then asked to volunteer snippets of information on the topic.

(It's all about ballooning, My mother went up in a hot-air balloon, They have a fire machine to make the balloon go up, Some balloons go on races, etc.)

This serves to get your students tuned in to the topic. Three things then happen. First, the reading becomes easier (they're expecting the words). Second, their comprehension is better, and third, recall is improved.

Blank-filling – The topic pages are teaching tools for you, so it's a good idea not to let your students fill in the blanks while you are going through the various sections of the page with them. The "pencils down" rule allows them to focus their whole attention on what you're saying. Later comes their turn for practice and activity by filling in the blanks and answering the questions on their own. The **Backing Sheet** can be used while you're teaching. For instance,

"Let's spell that word together. Now spell it silently, turn over the paper and see if you can write it down."

Teachers Notes

TOPIC PAGES

The **Topic Pages** have been designed for students who are experiencing difficulties with literacy. They aim to create a high level of interest which will appeal to students with low skill levels.

The **Topic Page** layouts have been tested in small remedial groups using an ACTIVE teaching mode which is outlined in the model below. Students were encouraged to fill in "blanks" in the **Topic Pages** only after teaching had taken place. The **Backing Sheet** was used during the teaching for students to write patterned, chunked and sight words from memory. Topics are arranged in themes and each page contains scope for your active teaching as follows:

Pre-reading
- Discovering pre-existing knowledge through discussion, with students volunteering snippets of information after looking at illustrations.

Reading
- Oral, group, silent, paired, or partner reading.

Word Study
- Phonic word patterns of regular words or theme words.
- Chunked words – words broken into chunks to assist blending and spelling rather than conventional syllables.

Comprehension
- Predicting.
- Cloze activity – to promote thinking and to reinforce word study items.
- Questions – literal and inferential.
- Main idea – creating or choosing titles.

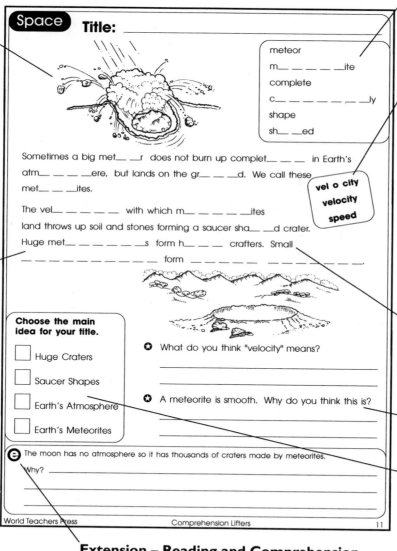

Extension – Reading and Comprehension
- Either a more difficult level of comprehension or more information on the topic.

Teachers Notes

BACKING SHEET

The **Backing Sheet** is provided for you to copy on the back of any or all of the **Topic Pages**. You'll notice that it is general and suitable for all **Topic Pages**. It is designed to complement your teaching and you may care to use or adapt the following suggestions as shown on the sample **Backing Sheet**.

Patterned Words

- Can be used while you're teaching or for practice afterwards.

Odd Words/Long Words

- Practice in reading and writing of longer words or sight words.

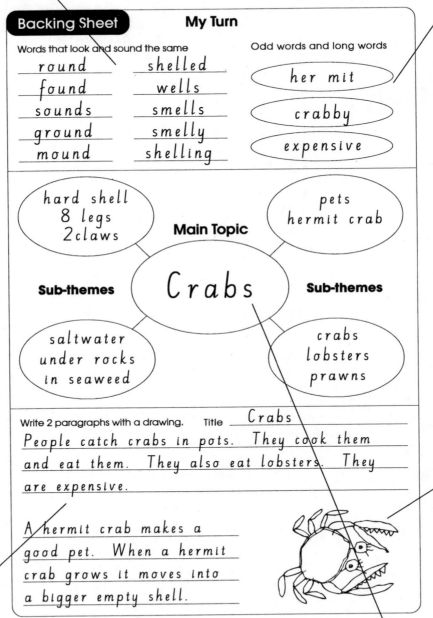

Backing Sheet

My Turn

Words that look and sound the same

round	shelled
found	wells
sounds	smells
ground	smelly
mound	shelling

Odd words and long words

- her mit
- crabby
- expensive

Main Topic

Crabs

hard shell
8 legs
2 claws

pets
hermit crab

Sub-themes

saltwater
under rocks
in seaweed

Sub-themes

crabs
lobsters
prawns

Write 2 paragraphs with a drawing.   Title   Crabs

People catch crabs in pots. They cook them and eat them. They also eat lobsters. They are expensive.

A hermit crab makes a good pet. When a hermit crab grows it moves into a bigger empty shell.

Drawing

- Matching drawing to main idea of story.

Writing

- Written (factual material) can assist students to write in a logical, thematic structure by giving them a standard format to formulate good habits.
- Later, format can be extended as basic skill improves and is wellfounded.

Integration

- Combining elements from text with pre-existing knowledge.
- Practice in sorting out random thoughts into sub-themes, lists, categories.

Backing Sheet

My Turn

Words that look and sound the same

Odd words and long words

_____ _____
_____ _____
_____ _____
_____ _____

Main Topic

Sub-themes

Sub-themes

Write two paragraphs with a drawing. Title _____

_____

_____

_____

_____

_____

_____

_____

Program Overview

Page	Subject	Word Study	Feature	Word Count
9	Space	soft "c"	main idea	58
10	Meteors	ing, igh	main idea	49
11	Meteorites	suffixes	main idea	47
12	Days of the Week	ough	main idea	52
13	Jupiter	ge, gi	main idea	53
14	Saturn	tch	true/false	55
15	Comet	contractions	who am I?	52
16	Galileo	ew	poor titles	53
17	Venus	i-e	sub-topics	57
18	Mars	ie	yes/no/doesn't say	55
19	Mariner 4	–	functions	42
20	Man on the Moon	ily	writing titles	50
21	Herschel	u-e	yes/no/doesn't say	65
22	Asteroids	oi	yes/no/doesn't say	54
23	Galaxies	ic	main topic	62
24	Space Probe	theme words	sequence	46
25	Montgolfier	o-e	inference	60
26	Space Junk	ly	listings	60
27	Infinity	ever	difficult concept	55
28	Observatory	theme words	inference	51
29	Astronaut Jokes	kn	word plays	46
30	Pathfinder	ce	details	62
31	Pathfinder Pictures	theme words	thinking ahead	59
32	Lunar Eclipse	wor	worst title	55
33	Solar Eclipse	wor	inference	60
34	Sun-A	theme words	difficult concept	67
35	Sun-B	theme words	inference	77
36	Distant Planets	ce	inference	72
37	Constellations-A	igh	good and poor titles	64
38	Constellations-B	ern	good and poor titles	63
39	Launch Sequence	theme words	sequence	60
40	Newton-Gravity	ew, ue	clues	74
41	Maria Mitchell	dis – cover – ed	good and poor titles	76
42	Fax from Shuttle	qua, wa	faxed letter	80
43	Life of a Star-A	ou	worst title	73
44	Life of a Star-B	gi, ge	worst title	70
45	Moon Jokes	wr	word plays	79
46	Letter from the Moon	ph	look for clues	79
47	To Live on Mars	abbreviations	sequence	84
48	Quiz	wh	review	N/A

Title: _____

ce
spa__ __
i__ __
__ __nter
sin__ __
pla__ __

Ever sin__ __ people have begun living on Earth, they have looked up at spa__ __.

What is out there in that vast pla__ __?

We can see the lights of stars and planets. We can see the sun, but mostly spa__ __ is emp__ __. Apart from specks of dust, small rocks and bits of i__ __, space has very little in it.

✪ Name some things in space.

_____, _____, _____

_____, _____, _____

✪ What do you think "vast" means? _____

_____

Think of a good title for the main idea.

_____

_____

Think of another one.

_____

_____

e If you could be a space traveler, what chance would you have of colliding with something? _____

_____

Title: _____

meteors

atmosphere

ȇ ing

gaze

gazing

make

mak__ __ __

fade

f__ __ __ __ __

become

becom__ __ __

igh

night

s__ __ __t

br__ __ __tness

m__ __ __t

When next you are gaz__ __ __ at the night sky, you might see a met__ __ __ mak__ __ __ its way across the darkness before f__d__ __ __ from sight.

Its brightness is caused by friction as the bit of rock or iron rushes through our atm__ __ph__re bec__ __ing white hot. We call them shooting st__ __s.

Pick the best of these titles and write it at the top of the page.

☐ Stargazing

☐ Rock or Iron

☐ Shooting Stars

☐ Atmosphere

✪ What do we call meteors? _____

_____

✪ Why do we call them that? _____

_____

_____

e Most meteors burn up and there is nothing left to fall on Earth.

Why does the meteor fade from sight? _____

_____

meteor

m__ __ __ __ __ite

complete

c__ __ __ __ __ __ __ly

shape

sh__ __ed

Sometimes a big met__ __r does not burn up complet__ __ __ in Earth's

atm__ __ __ __ere, but lands on the gr__ __ __d. We call these

met__ __ __ites.

vel o city

velocity

speed

The vel__ __ __ __ __ with which m__ __ __ __ __ __ites

land throws up soil and stones forming a saucer sha__ __d crater.

Huge met__ __ __ __ __ __ __s form h__ __ __ craters. Small

__ __ __ __ __ __ __ __ __ __ __ form __ __ __ __ __ __ __ __ __ __ __.

Choose the main idea for your title.

☐ Huge Craters

☐ Saucer Shapes

☐ Earth's Atmosphere

☐ Earth's Meteorites

✪ What do you think "velocity" means?

_____

_____

✪ A meteorite is smooth. Why do you think this is?

_____

_____

e The moon has no atmosphere so it has thousands of craters made by meteorites.

Why? _____

_____

_____

Space   Title: _____

ough

th__ __ __ __

thr__ __ __ __

th__ __ __t

__ __ __ __t

or ig in ally

originally

Some days of the week were named after objects in the sky.

For instance, Sunday was na__ __ __ after the sun. It was sun's d__ __.
Saturday was originally called Saturn's day, though the "n" and "s" have
now been dropped.

Monday was orig__ __ __ __ __ __ moon's day and thro__ __ __ the
ages the spelling has changed.

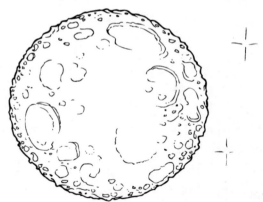

Think and come up with a good title for the main idea.

_____

_____

_____

_____

★ Saturday was named after the sun.

| True | False | Doesn't say |

★ How was Monday originally written?

_____

★ We ought to call Sunday...

_____

e Mars was the God of War and is a planet.

Which month is named after Mars? _____

Space **Title:** _____

ge	gi
hu__ __

__ __ant

lar__ __

lar__ __st

ima__ __ne

Jupiter is the fifth planet from the sun. It is hu__ __ and is often called a

gi__ __ __ planet. It is the lar__ __st planet in the Solar Sys__ __ __.

Ima__ __ __ __ a planet ten times lar__ __r than Earth and three hundred

t__ __ __s heavier! That is __ __ant Jupiter.

Jupiter has four lar__ __ moons and many smaller ones.

★ Why is Jupiter called a giant planet?

_____

_____

Pick the best title.

☐ Heavier than Earth

☐ Solar System

☐ Jumbo Jupiter

☐ Four Large Moons

★ Write the names of some of the planets that are
smaller than Jupiter.

_____

_____

★ Jupiter has twenty moons.

| True | False | Doesn't say |

e Jupiter is made up of a small, rocky core and swirling gases and liquids. How is
that different from Earth? _____

_____

Title: _____

tch

ca__ __ __

stre__ __ __

ma__ __ __es

ske__ __ __ing

scope

tele

telescope

known

Saturn is best k__ __ __n for its rings, which ca__ __ __ the light. They look stunning through a tele__ __ __pe.

The rings stre__ __ __ for about 200,000 km across and are made of rock and ice. People enjoy ske__ __ __ing Sat__ __ __ with its rings and about twenty m__ __ns.

Saturn almost ma__ __ __es Jupiter in size and is the second larg__ __ __ pla__ __ __.

✪ Saturn is the (largest, 2nd largest, 3rd largest) planet.

✪ Saturn is best known for its many moons.

| True | | False |

✪ Try sketching Saturn.

Pick a title.

☐ 200,000 km of Rings

☐ Stunning Saturn

☐ Telescopes

☐ Moons and Rings

e The rings could have been pieces left over when Saturn was forming, or maybe a moon came too close and broke up. What do you think? _____

_____

_____

Title: _____

I'm = I am

there's = _____ _____

it's = _____ _____

don't = _____ _____

won't = _____ _____

I'll = _____ _____

I've = _____ _____

Who am I?

I'__ in the sky but you wo__'__ see me often.

I do__'__ come into your sky every day or every month. Sometimes it'__ years between my visits.

There's not much of me. I'__ mostly rock, gas and ice. I'__ __ appear as a bright light and I'__ __ got a tail.

Draw me.

✪ I'm a _____.

✪ What am I made of?

_____

_____

ⓔ Comets have a long orbit around the sun. That's why we don't often see them, they're usually too far away.

Title: _____

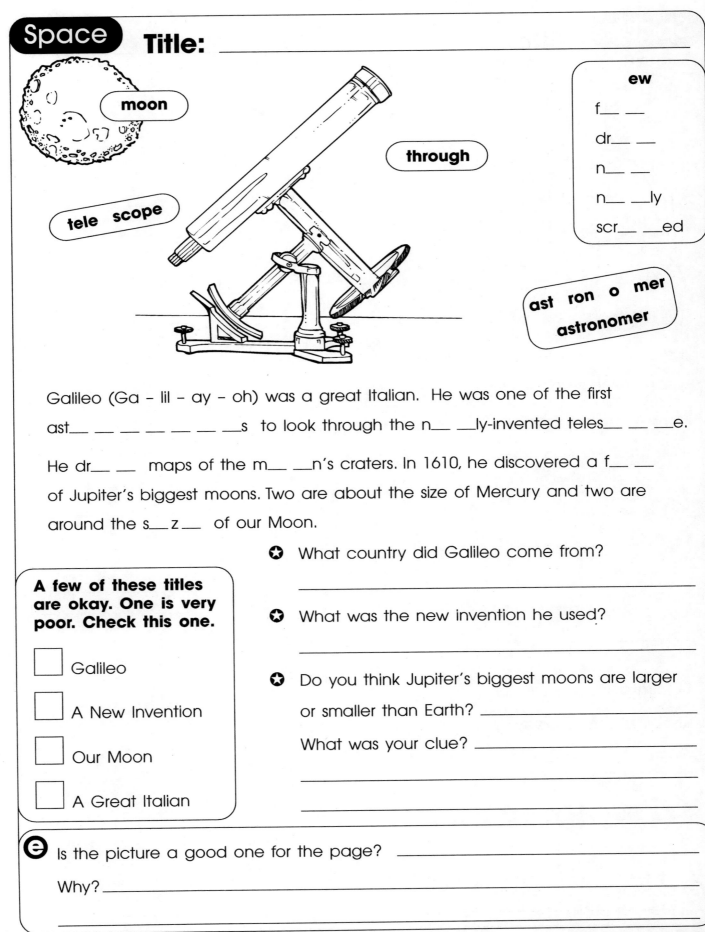

moon

tele scope

through

ast ron o mer
astronomer

ew

f__ __

dr__ __

n__ __

n__ __ly

scr__ __ed

Galileo (Ga – lil – ay – oh) was a great Italian. He was one of the first

ast__ __ __ __ __ __ __s to look through the n__ __ly-invented teles__ __ __e.

He dr__ __ maps of the m__ __n's craters. In 1610, he discovered a f__ __

of Jupiter's biggest moons. Two are about the size of Mercury and two are

around the s__z__ of our Moon.

A few of these titles are okay. One is very poor. Check this one.

☐ Galileo

☐ A New Invention

☐ Our Moon

☐ A Great Italian

✪ What country did Galileo come from?

_____

✪ What was the new invention he used?

_____

✪ Do you think Jupiter's biggest moons are larger

or smaller than Earth? _____

What was your clue? _____

_____

_____

e Is the picture a good one for the page? _____

Why?_____

_____

Comprehension Lifters – Book 3   World Teachers Press®

Title: _____

dif fer ent
different

Mercury
Venus
Earth
Sun

i – e

like

f__v__

s__z__

l__f__

t__m__s

The planet most l__k__ our Earth is Venus. It's about the same s__z__ as Ear__ __ and it has about the s__ __ __ mass. It comes closer to E__ __ __ __ than any other pla__ __ __.

Venus is different in that it has no moon and is about f__v__ t__m__s hotter than E__ __ __ __. We don't think there is any l__f__ on Ve__ __ __.

✪ Venus and Earth are about the same size. | True | False |

✪ How is Venus different from Earth? _____

_____

✪ What does "mass" mean? _____

_____

Venus is the main subject of the page. What are the two sub-topics?

_____

_____

e Venus is always shrouded in thick clouds so we can't _____

_____

_____

_____

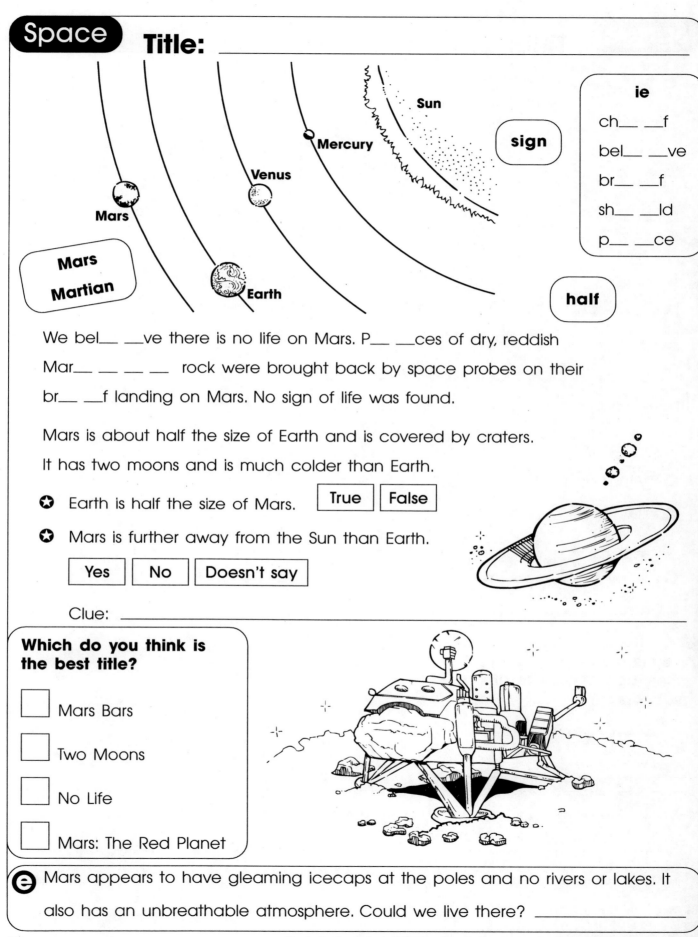

Space

Title: _____

ie

ch__ __f

bel__ __ve

br__ __f

sh__ __ld

p__ __ce

sign

half

Mars
Martian

Sun

Mercury

Venus

Mars

Earth

We bel__ __ve there is no life on Mars. P__ __ces of dry, reddish

Mar__ __ __ __ rock were brought back by space probes on their

br__ __f landing on Mars. No sign of life was found.

Mars is about half the size of Earth and is covered by craters.

It has two moons and is much colder than Earth.

✪ Earth is half the size of Mars. | True | False |

✪ Mars is further away from the Sun than Earth.

| Yes | No | Doesn't say |

Clue: _____

Which do you think is the best title?

☐ Mars Bars

☐ Two Moons

☐ No Life

☐ Mars: The Red Planet

ⓔ Mars appears to have gleaming icecaps at the poles and no rivers or lakes. It

also has an unbreathable atmosphere. Could we live there? _____

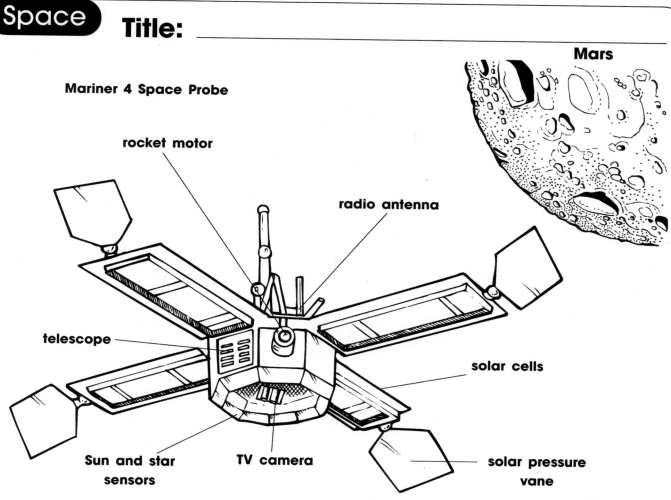

Mariner 4 Space Probe

- rocket motor
- radio antenna
- telescope
- solar cells
- Sun and star sensors
- TV camera
- solar pressure vane
- Mars

About thirty years ago, Mariner 4 was the first space probe to reach M__ __ __.
It sent back twenty-one pictures to Earth by radio.

✪ Fill in the blanks. Do the easy ones first, then go back and fill in the rest.

The _____ was used to help alter the probe's course.

The _____ helped it find the right direction.

The _____ took pictures.

The _____ made objects look larger.

The _____ recharged the batteries.

The _____ was used for sending and
receiving messages from Earth.

The _____ caught the *wind* from the Sun, to give control.

e Mariner 4 was carried by a powerful launching rocket from Earth. It was then thrust
on its path towards Mars.

Title: _____

x ily

happy

happily

easy

__ __ __ __ __ __

lucky

__ __ __ __ __ __ __ __

space

surface

1969 was an important year. Two people from Earth actually set foot on the

Moon's surf__ __ __.

The luck__ astronauts were Neil Armstrong and Edwin "Buzz" Aldrin. They wore

spa__ __suits so they could breathe eas__ __ __ and walk about safe__ __.

They had fun jumping so much higher than they could on Earth.

Think of two good titles. Write the best one at the top of the page.

_____

_____

_____

_____

⭐ Which year did the first person

step on the Moon? _____

⭐ Why did they wear spacesuits?

_____

_____

_____

_____

e The Moon is smaller than Earth and has much less mass, so the gravity is weak. This

means you can jump a long way on _____.

ast ron o mer

astronomer

Uranus

built

tele scope

u - e

huge

s__r__

__s__d

__sing

__s__ful

pict__r__

An astr__ __ __ __ __r is someone who studies the stars. William Herschel

(Her shell) was born in Germany about 250 years a__ __ and worked in Britain.

He was s__r__ he had seen a new planet, as he built a h__g__

tele__ __ __ __ __ on wheels and __s__d it to find the distant planet

Ur__ __ __ __. He also made a map of the Milky Way us__ __ __ the

tele__ __ __ __ __ he had built.

Think of two good titles for this page.

_____

_____

_____

✪ What's in the picture?

_____

✪ William Herschel was born in 1750.

| Yes | No | Doesn't say |

✪ Which word means "far away"?

_____

e What were Herschel's two most important achievements?

_____

_____

_____

Title: _____

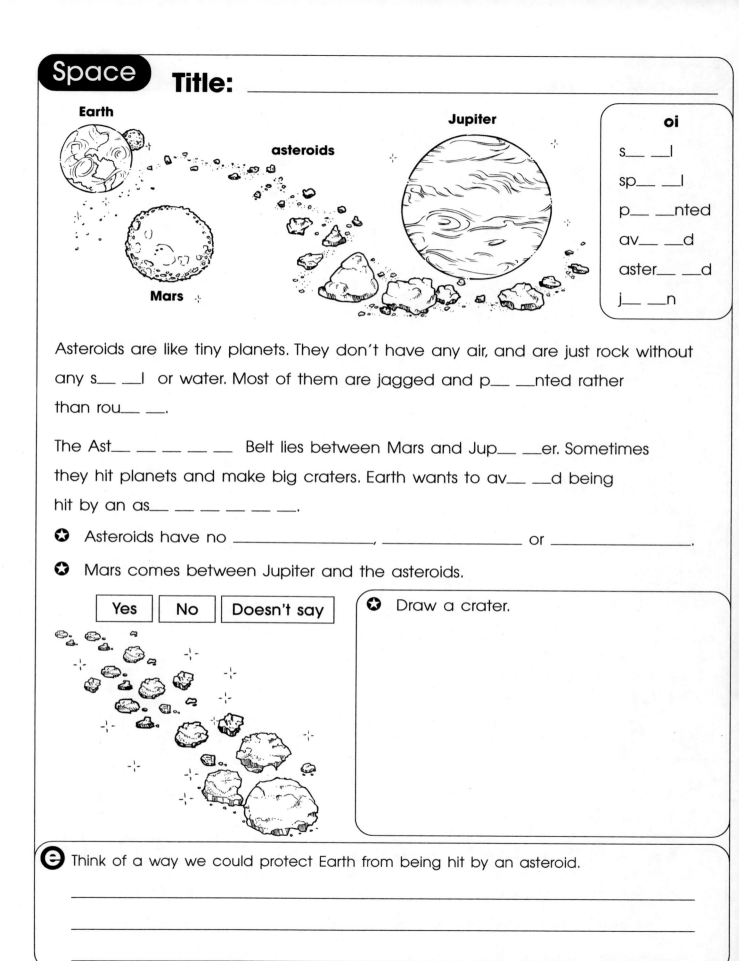

Earth

Jupiter

asteroids

Mars

oi
s__ __l
sp__ __l
p__ __nted
av__ __d
aster__ __d
j__ __n

Asteroids are like tiny planets. They don't have any air, and are just rock without

any s__ __l or water. Most of them are jagged and p__ __nted rather

than rou__ __.

The Ast__ __ __ __ __ Belt lies between Mars and Jup__ __er. Sometimes

they hit planets and make big craters. Earth wants to av__ __d being

hit by an as__ __ __ __ __ __.

✪ Asteroids have no _____, _____ or _____.

✪ Mars comes between Jupiter and the asteroids.

Yes	No	Doesn't say

✪ Draw a crater.

e Think of a way we could protect Earth from being hit by an asteroid.

_____

_____

Title: _____

our sun

galaxy

ic
top___ ___
mag___ ___
gigant___ ___
galact___ ___
part___ ___ular
traff___ ___
part___ ___les

A galaxy is just a huge collection of stars. There are many gigan___ ___ ___ galaxies in sp___ ___ ___. It's called the galact___ ___ system.

Our part___ ___ular galaxy is called the Milky Way. Our sun is near the edge of the galaxy which is why we see a band of millions of stars when we look one way, but fewer when we look the other way.

✪ Our galaxy is called _____.

✪ What is a galactic system? _____

_____

✪ Why do we see a band of stars? _____

_____

What is the main top___ ___ of this page?

_____

_____

_____

✪ What does the shape of a galaxy remind you of? _____

_____

_____

ℯ Apart from stars and planets, there are clouds of gas and solid particles in outer space.

Sometimes we can't see certain stars because _____

_____

Title: _____

outer
space

space
probe

Earth

space probe

traveled

tra__ __ __ing

Pluto

Jupiter

Saturn

In the 1980s a space pr__ __e trav__ __ed all the way

to the plan__ __ Pluto and then into outer space.

It flew past Sat__ __n, the ringed planet, on the way. When it first left Earth,

it made for the giant pl__ __ __t Jup__ __er, before trave__ing

on to Sat__ __ __ __.

**Put these in the order they happened.
(Not just the order they were written.)**

[ ] Flying past Saturn

[1] Starting by rocket from Earth

[ ] Reaching Pluto

[ ] Traveling on to outer space

[ ] Passing Jupiter

First _____

Second _____

Third _____

Fourth _____

Fifth _____

e What do you think might have happened next?

_____

_____

_____

Title: _____

First flight in 1783

o – e

sm__k__

r__p__s

v__t__

th__s__

h__l__s

r__s__

h__p__d

France

More than 200 years ago, two brothers in France sewed a huge balloon together. There were lots of r__p__s to hold the bits toge__ __ __ __. The bal__ __ __ __ was mostly made of paper.

In th__s__ days people thought that sm__k__ lifted ba__ __ __ __ns, so the brothers lit a f__ __ __ and filled the b__ __ __ __ __n with s__ __ __e.

The brothers had a long name – Montgolfier (Mont golf ee ay).

Vote for the best title.

☐ Two Brothers in France

☐ First Balloon Flight

☐ An Exciting Day in 1783

✪ When did the Montgolfier brothers first fly their balloon? _____

✪ What was the balloon made of?

_____

✪ What were the ropes for?

_____

e The balloon actually rose into the air because of the hot air from the fire (rather than the smoke). Why did they think smoke made it rise? _____

_____

Title: _____

Space seems to be comp__ __ __ __ __ __ empty.
There's no air and it's real__ __ cold. But it's not
absol__ __ __ __ __ empty. There are small bits
of rock and tiny pockets of frozen gas.

Now there is "space junk." Just as we have litter on
Earth, there are bits and pieces of spacecraft and
parts of rockets orbiting the S__ __ or drift__ __ __
in space.

add "ly"

complete__ __

total__ __

absolute__ __

real__ __

not totally empty

Sun

bits and pieces

space junk

⭐ Is space completely empty?

_____

⭐ What is in it? _____

_____

_____

Think of two titles.

_____

_____

_____

e Sometimes sections of discarded rockets fall back to Earth. The friction from our atmosphere
makes them red- or white-hot like meteors. How could these be dangerous?

_____

_____

Title: _____

∞
infinite
_ _ _ _ _ity

∞

ever
n_ _ _ _
for_ _ _ _
_ _ _ _y

4,500 +1

1,2,3,·········

2,345,789,320 +1

∞

5 TRILLION AND ONE

What is in_ _ _ity? Infin_ _ _ has no end. It goes on for_ _ _ _.

We think space is in_ _ _ite. If you traveled in a sp_ _ _craft on and

on, your craft would n_ _ _r get to the end.

∞
**the sign
for infinity**

Numbers are inf_ _ _ _e too. When we are

count_ _ _ we can get to huge num_ _ _ _

but we can always add on another nu_ _er.

✪ See if you can explain an "infinite number."

_____

_____

✪ If you traveled forever in a spacecraft, would you ever get to the end of

space? _____

**"Infinity" would be a good title.
Can you think of another?**

_____

_____

∞

e Infinity is very hard to accept. All the things we see have ends and edges, the
classroom, the street, the state we live in. Infinity has no boundaries, no finishes, no ends.

Space

Title: _____

observatory

revolving
rotating
galaxy
galaxies
telescopes

An obser_ _ _ _ _ _ is a place where there are large

tele_ _ _ _ _ _ for looking at the night sky. Usually they are on hills

and they have a rev_ _ _ _ _g domed roof which can open.

Inside, the huge tele_ _ _ _ _ can swing

up, down or around to follow the path of a star,

plan_ _ or gal_ _ _.

Select the best title.

☐ Following a Star

☐ Huge Telescopes

☐ Galaxies

☐ A Place for Watching Stars

☐ On a High Hill

✪ What is an observatory for? _____
_____
_____

✪ Why do you think they are built on hills?
_____
_____

✪ The telescopes can swing all ways.
Why? _____
_____
_____

e Telescopes are hooked up to computers so all the data can be recorded and

analyzed for later study. Why? _____

_____

_____

Title: _____

ast ro naut

friends

kn
__ __ees
__ __ot
__ __ow
__ __ew
__ __ock
__ __ife
__ __obby

Here are some jokes your fr__ __ __ds may not __ __ow.

James and Fred were in a two-man spacecr__ __t. James set off on a sp__ __ __walk with a lifeline __ __otted around his waist. An hour later, Fred heard a "__ __ock, __ __ock" on the door. "Who's there?" he asked.

✪ Why is this a silly story? _____

_____

_____

_____

Answers
- Planet of the Grapes.
- At launch time.
- An astronut.
- A star trek.

What is purple and __ __obby in space?

_____

When do astronauts have something to eat?

_____

_____

Think of a good title and write it at the top of the page.

ⓔ What do you call a crazy spaceman? _____

What is another name for a spacewalk? _____

Title: _____

battery
batteries

ce
boun__ __d
on__ __
surfa__ __
fa__ __
__ __lebration
Independen__ __

1997 was a great year for Mars. On July 4, the Pathfinder probe

bou__ __ __ __ on its air bags to a standstill on the surf__ __ __ of Mars.

On__ __ landed, it sent a faint message to say all was well. Then it

opened its met__ __ pet__ __s to fa__ __ its solar panels to the

sun to charge its bat__ __ __ __ __ __.

Pathfinder had traveled 500 million kilometers.

metal petals

standstill

✪ On what date did Pathfinder land?

_____ (month) _____ (day) _____ (year)

✪ What were the metal petals for? _____

_____

Your two titles, please.

_____
_____
_____
_____

✪ Why do you think it needed batteries?

_____
_____
_____
_____

ⓔ July fourth is Independence Day. The celebration in 1997 was not only for
the nation's birthday, but also for Pathfinder's achievement.

Title: _____

robot
Sojourner
pictures
color

Sojourner

Pathfinder sent many color p__ __t__ __es of the surf__ __ __ of Mars back to Ea__ __ __. Everyone in the world was amazed that the pic__ __ __ __ __ were so clear. We could see the red col__ __ of the surface and the large gray roc__ __ casting dark shadows.

The six-wh__ __led robot "Soj__ __ __ __ __ __" then set off over the r__ __ky surf__ __ __ to send back more pic__ __ __ __ __.

✪ What did Pathfinder send back to Earth?

_____

✪ Why were people amazed? _____

_____

✪ Why do we want pictures of Mars? _____

_____

_____

_____

This time, write a good title and a poor one.

_____
_____
_____
_____

🅔 Also in 1997 another probe called "Surveyor" was put into orbit around Mars to map the entire planet. What do you think is our next step for Mars? _____

_____

_____

Title: _____

> **Show me how a lunar eclipse works, Dad.**

re flect

reflect

wor

words

_ _ _ _ks

_ _ _ _king

_ _ _ _ld

_ _ _ _se

_ _ _ _st

First I'll draw our w__ __ld, the Earth. Then I'll d__ __ __ a bit of the Sun where the light comes from to make moonlight.

An eclipse of the Moon, or lunar eclipse, w__ __ks like this. The Moon travels into the shadow cast by the Earth. Now the Moon is dark and can't reflect the Sun's light.

Mark the worst title.

☐ Rocket to the Moon

☐ The Moon Disappears

☐ A Lunar Eclipse

✪ This shows an eclipse of the Sun.

| True | False |

✪ What makes the Moon shine?

_____

_____

e It looks as though there would be lots of lunar eclipses but the Moon is seldom exactly in line – it can be above or below the shadow and still shine.

Title: _____

Moon

Sun's corona

wor

___ ___ ___ms

___ ___ ___th

___ ___ ___ship

___ ___ ___shipped

___ ___ ___ry

___ ___ ___ ___ied

noc tur nal

nocturnal

A solar eclipse is an ec__ __ __ __ __ of the Sun. It happens during the day when the M__ __n passes between the Ear__ __ and the Sun.

It becomes very dark, like night, and some nocturnal animals come out. Even w__ __ms come to the surface.

In the old days, when people w__ __shipped the sun, they w__ __ __ied that an ec__ __ __ __ __ would bring a disaster.

Moon
shadow

E_____

Sun

M_____

✪ A solar eclipse is an eclipse of the Moon.

| True | False |

✪ We are told **not** to look at the Sun during an eclipse. Why?

_____

_____

_____

Solar means of the S__ __.

Lunar means of __ __ __ __ __ __ __.

e Most solar eclipses are only "partial" eclipses, so only part of the Sun is hidden. A "total" eclipse means _____

_____

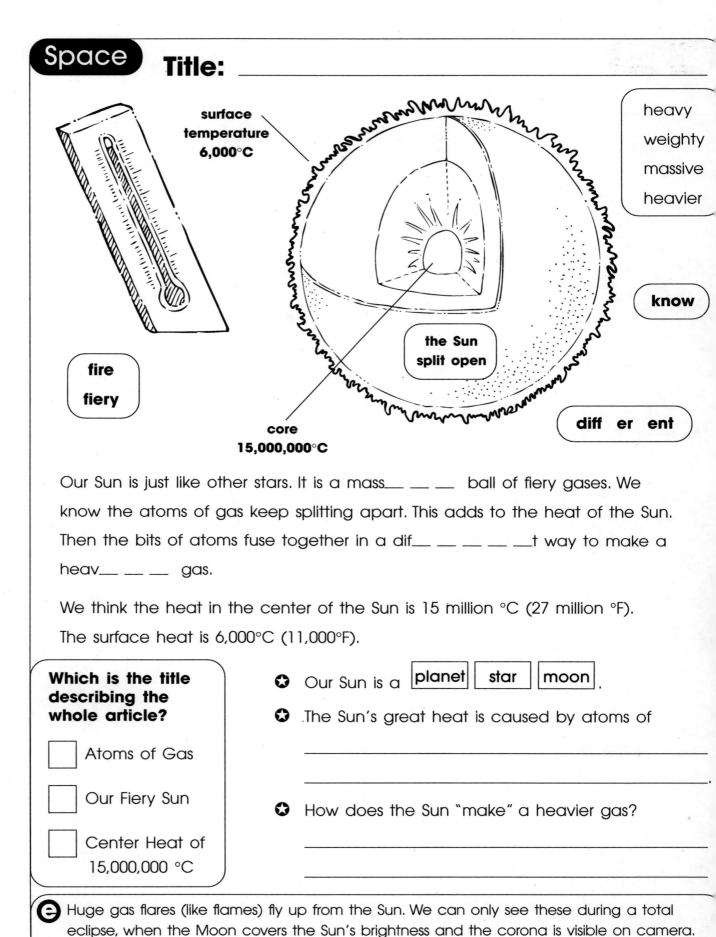

Space **Title:** _____

surface
temperature
6,000°C

heavy
weighty
massive
heavier

know

fire
fiery

the Sun
split open

diff er ent

core
15,000,000°C

Our Sun is just like other stars. It is a mass__ __ __ ball of fiery gases. We
know the atoms of gas keep splitting apart. This adds to the heat of the Sun.
Then the bits of atoms fuse together in a dif__ __ __ __ __t way to make a
heav__ __ __ gas.

We think the heat in the center of the Sun is 15 million °C (27 million °F).
The surface heat is 6,000°C (11,000°F).

**Which is the title
describing the
whole article?**

☐ Atoms of Gas

☐ Our Fiery Sun

☐ Center Heat of
15,000,000 °C

✪ Our Sun is a [planet] [star] [moon] .

✪ .The Sun's great heat is caused by atoms of

_____

_____.

✪ How does the Sun "make" a heavier gas?

_____

_____

e Huge gas flares (like flames) fly up from the Sun. We can only see these during a total
eclipse, when the Moon covers the Sun's brightness and the corona is visible on camera.

danger

d_ _ _ _ _ous

Sun

cover one lens

image

di rect ly

directly

image

binoculars
telescope
lens
focus
image

We can't look at the Sun directly and it's **dangerous** to look directly at it through

bin_ _ _ _ _ _ _ _ or tele_ _ _ _ _ _. So how can we see what it

looks like?

Do not look through the binoculars or telescope.

Point your bino_ _ _ _ _ _ _ or t_ _ _ _ _ _ _ _e at the Sun and

foc_ _ the im_ _ _ on to a white card. You will see a circle in which

there are dark spots. These are sun spots and they are cooler areas on the

Sun's surface.

✪ What can you use to see an image of
    the Sun?

_____ or

_____

✪ What are the dark areas on your image?

_____

_____

_____

**Focus your mind and write
two good titles.**

_____
_____
_____
_____

✪ Why are the spots darker? _____

_____

_____

ⓔ Even during an eclipse (when the Sun is half or totally covered) it is too dangerous to
look at the Sun. The rays can burn the back of your eye and make you blind forever.

Title: _____

ce

chan___ ___

distan___ ___

sin___ ___

poun___ ___

ice

icy

Neptune

Uranus has faint rings

Pluto, an icy cold planet

Some planets are too far away for you to have a chan___ ___ of seeing them with your naked eye. Even with a telescope they are hard to find at that great dista___ ___ ___. Uranus and Nept___ ___ ___ are both large plan___ ___ ___, about four times bi___ ___ ___ ___ than Earth. Ur___ ___ ___s has five moons and Nep___ ___ ___ ___ has two m___ ___ns.

Pluto is tiny. It is less than half the size of Ear___ ___ and does not have any moons.

⭐ How many moons?

Uranus _____ moons

Neptune _____ moons

Pluto _____ moons

Pounce on the best title.

☐ Naked Eye

☐ Uranus and Neptune

☐ Pluto

☐ The Outer Planets

✪ Is Pluto larger or smaller than Earth?

_____

✪ Uranus, Neptune and Pluto are icy cold planets. Why? _____

_____

_____

ℯ Mercury is a tiny planet and is nearest to the Sun. It is only about 50% bigger than our moon. You could spot Mercury low in the sky after the Sun has set in the twilight glow.

What is twilight? _____

_____

Comprehension Lifters – Book 3   World Teachers Pre

Title: _____

Leo
the lion

igh

h__ __ __

br__ __ __tness

n__ __ __tly

r__ __ __t

l__ __ __ting

sl__ __ __tly

Stars seem to make br__ __ __t patterns h__ __ __ in the

n__ __ __t sky.

For thousands of y__ __rs, people have given these clusters of l__ __ __ts

names and have made up stories about them.

There's Orion, the hunter. He has **three stars as a belt** and a **fuzzy cluster** as

a sw__ __ __ in his r__ __ __t hand. Leo, the lion, has **six br__ __ __t stars**

for his head and ne__ __.

✪ Clusters of stars make patterns in the sky.

| Yes | No | Doesn't say |

✪ Leo is the hunter.

| True | False |

Mark the good titles with a "g" and the poor with a "p."

☐ Patterns in the Sky

☐ Leo the Lion

☐ Clusters of Lights

☐ Six Bright Stars

sword

Orion
the hunter

✪ Make up a story about Orion.

_____

_____

_____

_____

_____

e These patterns or groups of stars are not actually close to each other. They just look close from our Earth. They appear to move across the sky maintaining their patterns over thousands of years.

Title: _____

con stell ation
constellation

North Star

nav ig ation
navigation

North

_ _ _ _ _ _ern

South

_ _ _ _ _ _ern

"Stella" is Latin for star. A group of stars is called a con_ _ _ _ _ation. From the north of our world, the con_ _ _ _ _ _ _ _ _ _ of the Great Bear points to the North Star. Ships used the North S_ _ _ to find their way in the old days.

From the south of our w_ _ _ _, the Southern Cross constellation was also used for nav_ _ _ _ _ _ _ before the compass was invented.

Mark the good titles with a "g" and the poor with a "p."

☐ Invention of the Compass

☐ Two Constellations

☐ North Star

☐ Navigation

✪ A southern constellation is _____
_____.

✪ The Great Bear is a
n_____
con_____.

✪ Why did sailors use stars? _____
_____
_____

e A "light year" is the distance that light travels in a year. The closest star to Earth is more than four light years away. Do you think it would be possible to travel to a star? _____

Why? _____

_____

Title: _____

our
module

rocket

em erg en cy
emergency

launch
module
excited
special

On the day of our laun__ __ into space, we were all exci__ __ __. Before

entering our space mod__ __ __, we were dressed in spec__ __ __ suits.

By that time, we had eaten a special meal.

Once we were in the spa__ __ module, we were strapped into our

la__ __ __h seats. Our training over many months had made us able to cope

with any emer__ __ __ __ __.

**Put these in the order they happened.
(Not the order in which they were written.)**

| 5 | Launching into space
(This one is done for you.) |
	Dressing in special suits
	Months of training
	Strapping into launch seats
	Eating a special pre-launch meal

First   _____

Second   _____

Third   _____

Fourth   _____

Fifth   Lau__ __ __ing into sp__ __ __.

e What do you think might have happened next? _____

_____

Title: _____

ew

n__ __

f__ __

gr__ __

N__ __ton

ue

cl__ __

bl__ __

gra vit y
gravity

think
thought

There is an old story about Newton, which happened more than 300 years ago.

It is said that Isaac N__ __ton was sitting under a tree with a f__ __ ripe apples. One fell and hit his head.

This made him think n__ __ thoughts and gave him a cl__ __. He th__ __ __ __ __, "Why did the apple fall down and not up into the bl__ __ sky? There must be a force pulling it." He called this force "gra__ __ __ __."

Check the poor title.

☐ Blue Sky

☐ Isaac Newton

☐ Force of Gravity

☐ A Pulling Force

Choose one to write at the top of the page.

✪ Where was Isaac Newton sitting? _____

_____

_____

✪ What was the weather like? _____

_____

_____

✪ What was your clue? _____

_____

e Newton realized that every body (star, planet, person) exerts a pull on every other body.

He realized that our moon stays near the Earth because of this f__ __ __e of

gr__ __ __ __ __ __.

Comprehension Lifters – Book 3 World Teachers Pres

Title: _____

dis   cover

disc__ __ __ __ed

d__ __ __ __ __ __ __y

1847

medal

Maria Mitchell grew up in the USA more than 150 years ago. After her work and studies were over in the evening, she loved to look through her father's tele__ __ __ __ __ at the stars and pl__ __ __ts.

One night in 1847, she saw a dim object with a tail, which she hadn't seen before. She raced to tell her fa__ __ __ __ that she had discov__ __ __ __ a new comet. The King of Denmark sent her a medal for her discov__ __ __.

A title tells what the whole story is about.

Make a ✔ at the poor titles and a ✗ at the good ones.

Write the title you think is best at the top of the page.

- [ ] 1847
- [ ] A Sky Watcher from Long Ago
- [ ] Maria Mitchell
- [ ] The King of Denmark
- [ ] Discovery of a New Comet
- [ ] A Lady Astronomer

After Maria Mitchell's comet discovery, she was invited to join an important group of scientists. She was the only female member.

Title: _____

Fax to:	630-555-3191	**Walter Smith**
Fax from:	847-555-0536	**Warren Jones**

6/25/99

Dear Walter,

We're so excited. We've both been chosen for the next space shuttle. We were up against q__ __lity astr__ __auts so we are "over the moon" (ha, ha, ha).

Our q__ __rters will be very sq__ __shed in the shuttle but everything is of top __ __ality – even the food.

We lift off on July 17 and link up with the Russian craft five days later.

We may be w__ __king on Mars! W__ __ch for us on TV!

With love,

Your astro__ __ __ __ cousins,

Wendy and Warren

qua

s__ __ __sh

__ __ __rters

__ __ __lity

__ __ __ntity

wa

__ __tch

__ __rren

__ __lter

__ __lking

__ __rm

⭐ This letter was sent by fax. | Yes | No | Doesn't say |

⭐ What does "over the moon" mean? _____

_____

⭐ When are Wendy and Warren leaving? _____ _____ 19_____

⭐ What do they hope to do? _____

_____

ⓔ Write a note back to them. Pretend you are Walter. Remember to put your fax number on the top and your full name. You can draw a picture on your fax to them.

Space   Title: _____

cloud of gas

expand grow bigger

white-hot star

ou

cl__ __dy
ar__ __nd
am__ __nt
ab__ __t
surr__ __nd

A star has a life span. It starts as a cl__ __d of gases and other bits in space.
These ga__ __s start pressing in and the cloud gets smaller and hott__ __. It
heats up until it glows white-hot. It is then a star and shines for ar__ __nd
100 million y__ __ __s.

The star then starts to ex__ __ __ __ until it's ab__ __t fifty times bigger.
It's then called a "red giant" and is an old star.

red giant

Check the worst title.

☐ A Star is Born

☐ Fifty Times Bigger

☐ From Youth to Old Age

☐ Life Span of a Star

✪ How does a star start life? _____

✪ When it expands, it is called a _____

✪ What does "life span" mean? _____

Most of the gas in the forming star is hydrogen. As it heats up, the hydrogen turns into helium. This produces more heat as the atoms are split. Some of this heat reaches Earth to warm us.

Title: _____

red giant

stable

un__ __ __ __ __ __

steady

un__ __ __ __ __ __

gi

__ __ant

ge

a__ __s

sta__ __

__ __nerally

hu__ __

chan__ __s

explode

__ __ __ __ __sion

supernova

A red __ __ant is an old star. Its hu__ __ size makes it

un__ __ __ble and __ __nerally red giants expl__ __ __. This

exp__ __ __ __ __ __ is called a "supernova" and is exciting to astronomers.

After the red __ __ant or supernova sta__ __, the star falls in on

itself and chan__ __s into a tiny star. The star in old a__ __ is

called a "white dwarf." The life span of a s__ __ __ covers

hundreds of millions of years.

white dwarf

Check the worst title.

☐ An Aged Star

☐ Life Span

☐ Stages in the Life
of a Star

✪ What is an exploding star called? _____

_____

_____

✪ Which is older, a white dwarf or a red giant?

_____

_____

✪ How long does a star live? _____

_____

e Number these in the correct order with the oldest last.

	red giant		white dwarf		gas cloud		supernova		star

Comprehension Lifters – Book 3 World Teachers Pres

Title: _____

wr

__ __ong

__ __ite

__ __estle

__ __ist

full moon

answers

Try these jokes.

W__ite your an__ __ __rs.

There are no "rights and __ __ongs."

Have fun __ __estling with them.

My ans__ __rs are at the bottom of this page.

✪ When is the Moon heaviest? _____

✪ How many balls of string would it take to reach the Moon? _____

_____

✪ When Neil Armstrong stepped onto the Moon, where did he stand? _____

_____

✪ What holds the Moon up? _____

Book titles. Explain the jokes.

Too Near the Sun by Yule B. Brown

 You'll be brown.
_____

Astronomy by I. C. Stars

_____

Moon Landing by Willie Makit

_____

Answers
- When it is full.
- Just one, but it would be very big.
- On his feet.
- Moon beams.

℮ Now you __ __ite a joke book title and author.

_____ by _____

March 25, 2075

Dear __ __ilip,

Well, we made it. Quite a trium__ __, don't you think? We landed on the Moon this morning and got into our bios__ __ere hotel. We can look at Earth.

We are going on a Moon Buggy tour tomorrow to see some of the lunar geogra__ __y (craters and ridges). We will wear spacesuits so we can breathe.

We'll be home in September.

Love, from Uncle Alf and Aunt Dee

PS You can __ __one or fax us here at:
     OO11 LUNAR 6660

ph
Philip
__ __ase
s__ __ere
geogra__ __y
trium__ __
__ __one
ne__ __ew

⭐ Are Aunt and Uncle working on the Moon or are they on vacatioin?

_____

Clue: _____

_____

⭐ What is "lunar geography"?

_____

_____

⭐ Can they breathe on the Moon?

_____

Clue: _____

_____

⭐ What date did they arrive?

_____

ⓔ Philip is the nephew. How do you know this? _____

_____

Title: _____

biosphere to live in
without spacesuits

First	1st
Second	_____
Third	_____
Fourth	_____
Fifth	_____

People think we could live on Mars if we made a few changes. F__ __ __t, we'd have to heat the planet so the polar icecaps would melt and Mars would have water for rivers, lakes, clouds and rain. Se__ __ __d, we'd have to make the atmosphere breathable.

Some ideas:

- Planting pine trees which grow in cold climates. They would help to change the atmosphere by giving out oxygen.

- Spraying black carbon on the icecaps so they would take in more heat from the sun and melt.

✪ Frozen water is in the Martian _____.

✪ Which trees would be planted first?

_____

Why? _____

_____

Your titles.

First _____

_____

Second _____

_____

Third _____

_____

🅮 Think of other ways to make Mars liveable. _____

_____

_____

answer

wh

__ __en

__ __at

__ __y

__ __ich

__ __ere

__ __o

Answer these questions.

Use the letters in the boxes to solve the puzzle below.

✪ Which planet has many rings around it? ☐(2) __ __ __ __ __

✪ Which day is named after the Moon? __ __ __ ☐(8) __ __

✪ What do we call travelers in space? __ ☐(9) __ __ __ __ __ __ __ __

✪ What is our galaxy called? __ __ __ __ __ __ __ ☐(1) __

✪ The spinning of the Earth makes __ ☐(7) __ __ __ and __ __ __ __

✪ What did Maria Mitchell discover? __ __ ☐(6) __ __ __

✪ What force makes apples fall down, not up? __ __ __ __ __ ☐(3) __

✪ Venus is between which two planets? __ __ ☐(5) __ __ and

__ __ __ __ __ __ __

✪ When the Moon passes between the Sun and the Earth, we have a

s__ __ __ __ ☐(4) __ __ __ __ __ __ .

ℯ Put the letters in the numbered squares into the boxes below.
The tiny planet-like objects are called:

☐ ☐ ☐ ☐ ☐ ☐ ☐ ☐ ☐
1   2   3   4   5   6   7   8   9